The Answers

that would appeal to your audience, backed up with examples. Here are some points you could include:
• Where this place is, what it is, how it looks, sounds, smells, feels etc.
• A short, informative account of your visit — when you went, what you did.
• Why you're recommending it — what its good points are, why others would like it.

Page 6 — Exam Technique

Q1 Purpose, audience and form.
Q2 a) • Stop look listen / pedestrian crossings / balls and other games in or near roads / need to be aware of vehicles / end with stop look listen again. Be inventive and fun to keep their interest.
b) • They've probably forgotten what it's like / the exam pressure / hormones / peer pressure / parental pressure to do well / uncertainty about the future. Use a bit of humour and lots of examples.
c) • My bedroom / looking through the keyhole, getting very small snapshots of the things in the room / Detail — books, photos / a shell from a beach holiday, an old toy / move on to more grown-up objects to show how my life has changed. Use senses to create atmosphere and feeling.
Q3 •

Spider diagram with centre "More choice at school" and branches:
- Students don't work hard because bored.
- Student morale would improve.
- School exam results would improve if students studied what they enjoyed.
- Students are nearly adults — need more responsibility.
- Counter-argument — students too young to know what subjects are best for them.
- How important is maths in real life anyway?

Q4 This is a speech aimed at teenagers, but you should still be fairly formal because you want to sound sophisticated to prove your point. The purpose is to argue, but you shouldn't just list points — you should try to make them as convincing as possible using writing techniques and interesting language. Here are some points you could include in your speech:
• How busy your daily routine is.
• What worries and stresses you have, especially ones that you think didn't affect students 30 years ago.
• How you're treated by adults.
• How you feel about important issues.
• Comparison with life of adults to show how you have it harder / are just as intelligent / should be treated with more respect.

Page 7 — Exam Technique

Q1 • Last Thursday was the long-awaited performance of our school musical. It was Grease and I'd struck it lucky at audition, landing the starring role of Danny. But on the day of the dress rehearsal disaster struck in the form of laryngitis, rendering me speechless, literally. My parents rallied round, plying me with cough syrup, but to no avail. I croaked my way through the performance, my understudy standing in for most of it. I was devastated at the thought of missing my debut, and went to bed miserable. I awoke on Thursday still feeling a bit groggy but on the mend and by the performance I had made a complete recovery. The play was an outstanding success.
Q2 a) • The Gothic stone building turns its blank, forbidding face to us as we approach. The lead-mullioned windows reflect the moonlight, showing us ourselves again, hiding the personality of the building within. Shadows loiter at the base of the walls; pitch-pools of uncertain depth. We skirt them nervously and approach the door.
b) • So ultimately if a genie were to appear in front of me right now and ask me the question, I'd have no hesitation in saying that the person I'd most like to be is Terry Wogan. Stunning good looks, exceptional talent and charisma; there is simply no other choice.
Q3 In this essay you should write for the examiner, so keep it quite formal. It doesn't tell you the form, so just write a normal essay in paragraphs. It's an explaining question, so use lots of interesting vocabulary and remember to give reasons for all the points you make. Here are some points you could include:
• Who the famous person is, what they do, brief description of them.
• What qualities you like about them.
• In what way you'd like to be like them.

Page — Spelling and Punctuation

Q1 a) I jumped out of the taxi, narrowly missing a very large puddle by the kerb.
b) Keeley said she wanted an MP3 player, a pair of shoes and some more make-up.
c) As the boat glided past, its bright paint glinting in the sun, I was able to see the captain saluting me, his gold braid fluttering in the breeze.
Q2 a) It's easy to learn to ski if you're not afraid of falling.
b) We looked everywhere but we didn't find Rupert's ball or the ponies' carrots.
Q3 a) I didn't want to go; the leaden sky seemed too threatening to set out.
b) Have you ever wondered what it would be like to travel in time? It'd be fantastic!
c) You can come to my party as long as you bring an expensive present; stay until the end; clear up any spillages; hand round the peanuts and don't drink any alcohol.
Q4 Words spelt correctly are:
unnatural, disappear, immediately, occasional.
Words spelt incorrectly should be corrected to:
argument, necessarily, favourite, embarrassed, conscious, deceived, conscience.
Q5 a) This afternoon we're going to Scarborough where you can buy fish and chips.
b) I'd like to borrow your bike, if you're not using it today.
c) We're going nearer the stage, because I can't hear the band from here.

Section Two — Writing to Inform and Explain

Page 9 — Writing to Inform and Explain

Q1 The correct words, in the following order, are:
inform, something, opinion, detail, bored, language, sophisticated
Q2 A letter to your pen friend telling her about your town
Web page about different types of tractors

Answers

The Answers

Q3 The following statements should be circled: "Instructions for an MP3 player", "Set of road directions from Bangor to Richmond" and "Gallery guidebook telling you how Picasso did his paintings".

Q4 a) no
b) yes
c) yes

Page 10 — Audience and Form

Q1 a) • Reasonably well-educated adults who are interested in current affairs.
b) • Predicted GCSE results are coming out this week and guess what? Yep, that's right, it's *another* new record! Apparently the number of you getting five good GCSEs (A*-C) will go up from 53% to 57%. Wow! Well done to you all.

Q2 balanced, facts, convincing, one-sided, controversial points.

Q3 a) Subjective
b) Objective
c) Subjective

Page 11 — Structure and Techniques

Q1 a) • You can choose to view the animals from our monorail, which stands fifteen metres above the paddocks, and uses a unique silent gearing system so that you can watch the animals in peace and quiet.
b) • There are hundreds of species of animals which visitors will see. There are lots of places for refreshments, from snacks to full meals. You can drive through many of the animal enclosures in your car.

Q2 a) subheadings
b) clearly, details
c) examples

Q3 a) To direct the reader through your points
b) To make yourself sound knowledgeable on a subject
c) To engage the reader by provoking a reaction
d) To make your writing less boring for the reader

Page 12 — Writing Your Own

Q1 a) • The subheading tells the reader what the text beneath it contains. This helps the reader decide whether or not they want to read it.
b) • Looking for top quality laboratory facilities?
c) • QEGS prides itself on sporting success, and we frequently compete at national level. Our indoor sports hall, Olympic size pool and array of floodlit all-weather pitches provide for most sporting activities, rain or shine.

Q2 • My life is really difficult. I work in a mill for twelve tedious, hard hours six days a week. There's no chance of me being able to go to school or spend time with my friends. The mill is so noisy I always have a headache, and it's dangerous too — last year one of my friends lost an arm.

Q3 You're writing a letter to a friend, so make sure you start it and end it correctly. Your tone should be fairly informal. A good answer to this question would probably include:
• Information about the memorable event, e.g. when and where it took place, what happened and who was there.
• An interesting account of how the event made you feel and why you have remembered it since your childhood.
• Some descriptive techniques to make your writing more impressive — interesting vocabulary and imagery.

Q4 You're writing a speech, so make sure you have a good introduction and conclusion. A good answer for this question might include some of the following points:
• An explanation of a job that you'd like to have when you're 25.
• An explanation of what you'd like your home life to be like; marriage, single, homeowner, children etc.
• An explanation of any hobbies or sports you'd like to be involved in.

Page 13 — Writing Your Own

Q1 • This morning I was awoken from my restful sleep by beautiful birdsong and the sun shining through my curtains. It was such a lovely morning I leapt out of bed and dressed as quickly as I could so that I could make the most of this gorgeous day.

Q2 • At the tender age of seven I lived in a beautiful seaside town called Bridlington. Despite the bleak, arctic winters with their biting winds and icy rain, it was a charming locality. I spent countless blissful hours frolicking at the water's edge and frittering away my meagre allowance at the amusement arcades. When my family made the impulsive decision to relocate to Scunthorpe, I departed my childhood playground with a heavy heart.

Q3 a) • I'd really like to meet Dame Ellen MacArthur because she's someone that I really admire. I'd like to ask her how it felt to break the record for sailing single-handed non-stop around the world, and how she dealt with the loneliness during her trip.
b) • I was really nervous when I took my grade six flute exam because I'd been struggling with one of the set pieces and I hadn't managed to play it all the way through without making a mistake.

Q4 You're writing a newspaper article, so make sure that you write in a suitable style. A good answer might include some of the following points:
• Exam boards should ensure that their specifications are equally attractive to boys and girls.
• Incentives could be offered to students who do well.
• Careers advisors could be brought into schools to emphasise the importance of academic achievement.
• Parents and teachers could try to tackle the attitude amongst underachieving pupils that it's not cool to do well.

The Answers

Section Three — Writing to Describe

Page 14 — Writing to Describe

Q1 a) • You could write from your own point of view, walking through the wood, or as a small animal in the wood, or an owl, or as a tree.

b) • You could write from the point of view of a tourist, or as someone who lives in the destination.

Q2 a) • From the diving board, the swimmers below look like a shoal of brightly coloured fish, jumping and splashing.

b) • The noise in the pool has a strange, echoey quality, like whalesong.

c) • I feel the roughness of the tiles under my bare feet, and the smooth patches where someone has spilt their conditioner.

d) • The bitter chlorine catches in the back of my throat, mingled with the smell of sweaty feet and talcum powder.

Q3 a) • The sandy beach stretches out below me in the shape of a crescent, with gulls soaring above tiny white breakers. A small dinghy bobs peacefully on the surface of the azure water.

b) • The tall reddish cliffs mark the boundary between land and sea. The area is dotted with signs warning that the path has collapsed. As I get closer I can see little flowers on the cliff path. People pass each other carefully, holding the fence tightly.

c) • I can see a million tiny sparkling grains of sand. Little crabs are clambering in pools full of pebbles that look like semiprecious stones.

Page 15 — Imagery

Q1 a) simile
b) metaphor
c) simile
d) metaphor

Q2 a) • The car skulked past silently.

b) • The concrete pillars were tree trunks in the jungle of the city.

c) • Blood rushed to my face, giving me a bright red glow as if I had a rather bad rash.

Q3 a) • I was so excited I felt like I might burst like a jacket potato left in the microwave too long.

b) • The cave was a yawning mouth in the face of the mountain.

c) • The fire was a hungry tiger, consuming everything in its path.

Page 16 — Techniques

Q1 b) • As I ran headlong down the path, I didn't know whether Henry was following me.

c) • Although the beach seemed deserted, one solitary little boy was trawling aimlessly in the rock pools.

Q2 a) • summer; Screams ring out across the countryside beyond the park. A hot, greasy smell of hot dogs and sun cream is carried on the warm breeze.

• winter; Cold maintenance men clang nuts and bolts whilst rainwater gathers in pools on empty seats. As the days begin to get longer a feeling of expectancy grows; new coats of paint are applied and the park slowly begins to wake from its slumber.

b) • first day; I'm lost in a maze of corridors. The strong smell of disinfectant clings to my clothes; a faint whiff remains even when I've reached the safety and comfort of my own home.

• now; I saunter casually into the classroom and every single face is familiar. I'm bored of this place. I know every inch of it by heart, just like I know my own house. Nothing seems new or interesting.

c) • day; The strong fluorescent lights are throbbing beacons. People dash up and down the aisles like animals released from a zoo and the non-stop beep of the barcode scanner rings out.

• night; In the dingy light freezers hum their own tune, the only company for the watchman who thinks of his family tucked up at home. Rows of shadowy shapes stand on the shelves like frozen soldiers.

Page 17 — Writing Your Own

Q1 a) • You might find my choice of lunch date a little shocking.

b) • Imagine a place where all your senses are assaulted simultaneously by its exotic, outrageous and seductive nature.

c) • Today I celebrated my 250th birthday.

Q2 a) • It's 4pm. The doors burst open and floods of children pour out into the street, spilling over the edges of the pavements, engulfing passers-by in their tidal surge. They're free.

b) • When he smiles and tells me everything will be OK, I believe him. Completely.

c) • So as the train pulls slowly out of the tiny station, through the scattered pine trees, you catch a glimpse of the sand beyond. A small figure on the beach turns and waves, and at that moment you know that, one day, you'll be back.

Q3 This question doesn't give a specific audience so you should address the examiner in your mini-essay. Your language should be fairly formal and you should try to use an interesting style. Choosing an unusual place will probably make it easier to come up with something original.
A good answer to this question would probably include some of the following:
• A basic outline of where the place is, and how to get to it.
• An interesting description of what the place is like. A lot of this description will be visual but you'll get extra marks if you can refer to other senses e.g. sounds and smells.
• An explanation of why the place is important to you, for example a description of how it makes you feel or a special memory you have involving the place.
• Plenty of descriptive language techniques like imagery, and interesting vocabulary.

Q4 Again, there's no specified audience for this mini-essay so you should write for the examiner. Try to include as many personal details as possible, so the examiner feels that he / she is really finding out about the person you're describing.
A good answer might include some of the following:
• A description of what your friend looks like physically.

The Answers

- A description of your friend's temperament and their personality — e.g. their likes and dislikes.
- A description of any hobbies or activities your friend is involved in.
- Plenty of descriptive language techniques like imagery, and interesting vocabulary.

Section Four — Writing to Argue and Persuade

Page 18 — Writing to Argue and Persuade

Q1

Purpose	to argue
Form	letter
Audience	local council

Q2 a) healthier school meals
b) less air travel

Q3 a) • Buy the "Wizzitron 590" industrial cleaner.
b) • From a speech. It starts with "Ladies and gentlemen" which is a clear sign of a speech. Later it has other indications that people are gathered together listening to a speech such as "Thank you for attending" and "Today, you'll witness".
c) Business people. It says "your business' cleaning needs" and "save your business thousands".

Page 19 — Structure and Techniques

Q1 a) • Why should our children have to play in a rubbish dump?
b) • Tonnes and tonnes of rubbish have been dumped in our locality and everyone agrees that it's the most disgusting sight in the world.
c) • The council is forcing innocent, disadvantaged young children to play in areas that constitute a severe hazard to their health.

Q2 a) • Over 70% of year 11 students complained that there's no quiet place to study at school.
b) • In between lessons, I find myself at a loose end. I don't always have enough work to justify a trip to the library, and frankly sometimes I just want to relax.

Q3 a) • In previous years, there was plenty of time for sport, unlike the situation today. In the future I'd like to see every student with a choice of sporting activities available to them.
b) • In times gone by it was socially acceptable to go to India and "bag a tiger", but now most people no longer find such things acceptable. In years to come we will come to view activities such as fishing as barbaric torture.

Q4 This is a letter, so make sure you write one — start and end it properly. You're writing to the council which means you should be writing in a formal and serious style. Your purpose is to persuade, so use plenty of persuasive writing techniques. Statistics and emotive language would be appropriate, for example, but remember that you're writing to the council, so avoid some techniques like humour. Some points you could include are:
- Explain the seriousness of the problem (e.g. the amount of rubbish).
- State why it's such a problem (e.g. health problems).
- Say what you want them to do.
- Counter-argument — it would be expensive to deal with but you think it's justified.

Page 20 — Structure and Techniques

Q1 b) • Repetition (in threes). This is effective because it really emphasises the writer's point of view, making it more memorable to the reader.
c) • Quoting authorities. This is effective because it makes the point appear more trustworthy and believable.

Q2 b) • Uses flattery to encourage the reader to support the cause. Use of "yourself" and "your" to directly appeal to the audience.
c) • Emotive language. This is effective because it will evoke sympathy in the reader and might persuade them to donate money.

Q3 This is a magazine article, so you can use interesting subheadings and other presentational features such as bullet points. Your audience is teenage boys, so it's fine to use informal, chatty language. Remember to still use lots of impressive vocabulary though. Your purpose is to persuade, so you should use lots of writing techniques to help you get your point across. Unlike question 3 (writing to the council), it would be fine to use humour, sarcasm and even silliness here. Some points you could include are:
- How exercise is a great way to improve your health, and how this can improve your life, e.g. you're less likely to become ill.
- Exercise can be great fun and is a good way to socialise.
- How being healthy can save you money, e.g. if you don't smoke you can save hundreds of pounds a year.
- Being healthier will make you more attractive and energetic.

Page 21 — Writing Your Own

Q1 a) •

Presenting an argument	Developing an argument	Presenting a counter-argument
It is clear that / In my opinion	Also / Furthermore / In addition	On the other hand / Although some people argue that

Q2 a) final paragraph
b) second paragraph
c) first paragraph
d) third paragraph

Q3 a) form: speech, purpose: to persuade, audience: pupils at school
b) • Is one little chocolate bar going to kill us?
c) • A similar boycott in my cousin's school achieved results really quickly.
d) • We students used to feel as though we were important, as though our opinions mattered, but nobody consulted us over this; nobody cares about what we think.

Page 22 — Writing Your Own

Q1 a) • Good morning everyone. Thank you for coming to hear me speak about this very important issue. Today, I'm going to propose a zero-tolerance policy towards bullying. I propose that any student found guilty of bullying should be instantly expelled.
b) • Thank you for giving up your time to listen to my proposal. Taking all of my points into consideration, I urge you to reconsider the school's bullying policy. Together we can

The Answers

make the school a safer place for everyone.

Q2 You're writing a speech, so should write in a similar style to how you'd speak. The audience is your school, and although you will be talking to lots of students, remember that your argument is aimed at the teachers. This means your speech should be fairly formal and serious. You're writing to argue, so include plenty of writing techniques such as statistics, counter-arguments, rhetorical questions and emotive language to make your point more effective. Here are some points you could include:
- How serious bullying is.
- How the current anti-bullying policy is ineffective.
- Instant expulsion would act as a deterrent.
- Instant expulsion would remove the bullying problem by removing the bullies.

Q3 a) • Dear Mrs Patton,
I would like to draw your attention to the fact that many of our teachers expect us to produce word-processed homework, when a number of us lack the facilities to do so at home. As a solution to this problem, I would like to suggest that you allow us to borrow the school's laptops during the evenings.

b) • It's unfair and discriminatory that some students can get better marks than others just because they have a computer at home.
• The laptops aren't being used in the evenings at the moment so they wouldn't be missed.

c) • In conclusion, I believe that allowing students to borrow laptops would provide us with an equal chance at getting the top grades, which would improve morale, student self-esteem and the reputation of the school. I await your response with anticipation.
Yours sincerely,
Keeley McAndrew

Section Five — Writing to Advise

Page 23 — Writing to Advise

Q1 The following should be underlined:
Web page on how to conserve energy
Magazine article on interesting ways to save money
Problem page in a magazine
Leaflet on how to stop smoking

Q2 a) True
b) False
c) False
d) True
e) True

Q3 a) Informal
b) Formal
c) Informal

Q4 b) • I would recommend that you sold your car.
c) • My mate reckons you should give up your job.
d) • I wouldn't advise you to wed the first man that you meet.

Page 24 — Writing Style

Q1 a) • No. The tone is very formal and official, which is not appropriate for the teenage audience.

b) • The extract does not address the reader directly. It would have been more appropriate to address them directly, as the advice would seem more personal and relevant.

c) • It's exam time again, but don't panic! Here are some handy hints about how to stay calm for your revision. First, make sure you know what you've got to revise. It's no good reading your entire Biology textbook if you only need to know a chapter of it. Secondly, make yourself a revision timetable. It's a boring task, I know, but it will help you organise your time really well.

Q2 a) How to get here
b) What you should buy for your pet
c) Which way now?

Q3 How to live a longer life
Step 1 — Diet
Below are some important diet tips:
• Eat at least five portions of fruit and veg a day.
• Eat wholegrain bread and cereal.
• Drink eight glasses of water a day.
• Avoid fatty, salty and sugary snacks.

Page 25 — Structure and Techniques

Q1 b) • Next time you're about to take out the rubbish, go through it and see how many of the items you're throwing out are made of glass, metal, paper or plastic. These could all be recycled instead, which could reduce your waste by about half.

c) • Before your holiday, go on relevant websites and look at how much common items cost in euros. This will get you used to thinking about prices in terms of euros and will make it easier for you to work out how much things are really costing you.

Q2 The correct words, in the following order, are:
advise, tone, understand, directly, formally, informal

Q3 This time you're writing a speech, so remember to make it sound good spoken aloud, and refer to your audience directly. You're writing for teenagers, so you should write fairly informally. The purpose is to advise, so try to give out useful tips. Some points you could include are:
• Recycling paper, metal, glass and plastic.
• Using public transport and car sharing.
• Switching off electrical appliances and not leaving them on standby.
• Promoting renewable energy.
• Only buying wood products which come from sustainable forestry projects.

Page 26 — Writing Your Own

Q1 a) • The tone is informal and reassuring. The text's purpose is to help students feel calmer about starting at a new school, so this reassuring, friendly tone will help achieve this.

b) • The language used is chatty and colloquial at times e.g. "don't worry" which will appeal to the intended audience of school-age children.

c)
You'll settle in really quickly.
Form tutors really friendly.
A lot more freedom than primary school.
You must tell someone if you've got any problems.
Starting a new school
Use this handy map to find your way around.
Look at the noticeboards by the hall for school rules and useful information.

d) • On your first day when you get to the school gates, stop and take a few long, deep breaths. This'll help calm your nerves and make you feel better.

The Answers

e) • To sum it all up, starting a new school is a great opportunity for you. You'll expand your horizons and have loads of fantastic new experiences. It's normal to be nervous, but hey, life would be boring without a few nerves.

Q2 You're writing a leaflet, so it would be useful to include subheadings, bullet points etc. Your audience is young people, so you should be using appropriate informal, chatty language. Your purpose is to write a piece of advice, so remember to be reassuring, understanding and to give out helpful, practical suggestions. Some points you could include are:
• Finding someone nice to show you around initially.
• Joining clubs to meet new friends.
• Being yourself instead of putting on a show.

Section Six — The Exam

Pages 28-29 — The Exam Inform/Describe Questions

Answer 2: • This part of the answer would get grade A because it uses vivid and imaginative vocabulary, varied sentence structures and effective punctuation. It makes good use of alliteration and the rule of three. Some of the words are a bit tricky for children though.
To get a higher mark the writer would need to keep the target audience in mind all the way through the answer.

Answer 3: • This part of the answer would get grade C because it has a clear structure and the spelling and punctuation are mostly good. The writer also uses a mix of long and short sentences and a variety of sentence structures, but some of the sentences ramble a bit.
This answer would get a higher mark if it used more interesting vocabulary. Some imagery and more vivid descriptions would help too.

Answer 4: • This part of the answer would get grade A* because it is original and inventive. It employs three popular techniques for writing for children — repetition, rhythm, and the rule of three. The spelling and punctuation are accurate, and the vocabulary and sentence structures are varied. It even uses punctuation for humorous effect with the long list of hyphenated words.

Pages 31-32 — The Exam Argue/Persuade Questions

Answer 1: • This part of the answer would get grade A* because the writer has really captured the satirical tone that is used by many columnists. The writer responds to unfair generalisations about teenagers with humour, which makes them seem mature. The ideas are presented confidently and clearly and the writer has used techniques like rhetorical questions and lists of three well. The title is imaginative and interesting.

Answer 2: • This part of the answer would get grade B because the writer makes a number of valid points that relate directly to the question. Sentences follow on from one another in a logical manner and are smoothly connected. The spelling and punctuation are good, and the use of questions to draw the reader into the article is appropriate.
To get a higher mark the writer would need to develop each point more fully by giving examples and providing more detail, and use more varied vocabulary.

Answer 3: • This part of the answer would get a grade A because there is a smooth flow between the sentences and paragraphs. Contrasting sentence structures engage the reader, and the author's ideas are presented clearly and logically. The spelling and punctuation are both good too.
To get a higher mark this answer could use some even more ambitious vocabulary, engage more with opposing viewpoints, or present some more abstract ideas.

Answer 4: • This part of the answer would get grade A* because it conveys a convincing and well-structured argument. The author imaginatively relates the idea in the question to the exploitation of children in the past. The vocabulary is also spot on for a passionate opinion piece, e.g. "toxic", "allegedly democratic", and "preposterous". The sentence structures are both varied and complex, and language techniques have been used well.

Section Seven — Creative Writing

Page 33 — Writing About Moving Images

Q1 This is a film review so its purpose is to inform and persuade. Make sure you include factual information about the film as well as giving an opinion about whether it's good or bad. If you think it's good then you should use persuasive language to convince people to go and see it. Don't forget who your audience is — the review is for the school magazine so should be aimed at people your own age. Here are some points you could include:
• The title, length and rating of the film, plus the name of the director and starring actors
• The genre of the film — e.g. where and when it's set, whether it's an action film or a romance, whether it's live action or animated...
• A short summary of the plot
• Why you're recommending it — what its good points are, why others would like it.

Q2 This is the script for a voice-over, so write it in language that would sound good spoken aloud. You're not given a specific audience for this question, so just write for the marker. That means being fairly formal and avoiding colloquial language. Your purpose is to describe and inform, so use lots of interesting vocabulary and facts. You only have to write the beginning of the voice-over so you won't be able to do more than introduce your town. Some points you could include are:
• The name of the town
• Where your town is
• How many people live there
• Whether it's industrial, or touristy, or has a lot of commuters

Q3 • There's lots of visual detail about the setting for the director, e.g. the morning sun, the tendrils of mist, it's in a park near a river, there's no one else around.
• There's description of what the main character looks like and what she's wearing, e.g. she has long auburn hair and is wearing a summery cardigan.
• A flashback has been set up to the year before and there's more information about the time of day.

Q4 This is a script for an advert so you are trying to sell someone a product. The product is a biscuit so your language

The Answers

can be informal and chatty but should be persuasive. Decide what images will appear in the advert while the voice-over is happening. Some points you could include are:
- the name and type of biscuit
- what's so great about it — whether it comes in loads of flavours, or it's low fat or it's shaped like a dinosaur
- where people can buy it

Q5 This is a short story but it needs to have lots of detailed description in it to help the director. You should make it clear whether the story is happening at the present time or whether it's historical or futuristic. There should be a clear sense of place — the story could be set in a city or in the country. Your purpose is to entertain so make your characters distinctive and memorable so that your audience will care what happens to them.
- It was the height of summer, and in America's Deep South, the air was thick and hot. Memories of the Civil War were still fresh in the minds of the local communities, communities that were still recovering from the devastating losses of their husbands, brothers and sons. At 16, Emily Foster was too young to have lost a husband, but she had said goodbye to her father a year earlier. He hadn't returned. Everyone else seemed to accept that he had died in the war, but for Emily, something didn't add up...

Page 34 — Writing on a Particular Theme

Q1 •

[Mind map with "Colour" at centre, branches to: How colour affects mood — red for aggression and blue/green for calm; Colour and identity — racism?; Traffic lights — red, amber and green; Colouring books — child's crayons; Changing colours in autumn; What it's like to be colour-blind]

Q2 You need to decide on your characters and a rough plot before you start your answer. This is only an introduction so you don't need to plan in very much detail yet. You will use this introduction again for Q5 though so you do need to think ahead. It's worth making brief notes on what's going to happen in the beginning, build-up, climax and ending of your story. Some points to think about:
- Start with the line you're given — and make sure you've copied it exactly.
- Decide who (or what) the person is talking to, and what their reply might be
- Dialogue gives you a chance to establish your character(s) early so decide how they're going to speak

Q3 This is a magazine column so it could aim to entertain or to inform. The question doesn't say what type of magazine it is so keep your language fairly formal. You can also decide whether you are going to make it serious or humorous. There are lots of options here, you could:
- Adapt a personal anecdote to fit the title
- Make something up. You should write in the first person but you don't have to write as yourself — you could write as a character.

Q4 You can choose to write any type of creative text — it could be a speech, a script, an article, a review, a narrative piece... or something else. Choose any form that suits your idea. Whichever form you choose, always think about the audience and purpose of your text.

Q5 You'll have done some rough planning of the story for Q2, so use your notes to come up with a more detailed plan. As always, before you start you should make sure you know exactly what's going to happen for the beginning build-up, climax and ending of your story. Once you've written the story you should think about:
- Whether you've used a variety of styles — different sentence lengths and structures, and interesting vocabulary
- Whether your punctuation and grammar are correct
- Whether your spelling is spot on — double check difficult and unusual words

Page 35 — Changing the Genre of a Text

Q1 This is a newspaper article so it should be formal and informative. You should include as many details from the original poem as you can and use journalistic phrases to make your article more realistic. You could make up some suitable quotes to illustrate how people felt during or after the events of the poem. Don't forget to come up with a neat, snappy headline as well. Some points you could include are:
- When and where the events happened
- Who was involved in the events
- Were the events witnessed by lots of people
- What the effects of the events are / could be

Q2 You only need to write the beginning of the short story but you should include plenty of detail taken from the article. Your purpose is to entertain so you'll need to come up with interesting details to flesh out your plot. The article gives some details on some characters so use them to help you with ideas. Some things to think about are:
- When your short story is set — does it happen before, during or after the events described in the article
- Who your main characters will be — you don't have to use all the people mentioned in the article and you can make up some others

Q3 Choose the event from a text you know well so that you'll be able to include lots of detail. You're writing for a women's magazine so the style can be fairly informal and you can use chatty language. The main purpose of the text is to entertain, although it should also inform. Some things you could include are:
- Details of the event — what happened where and when, and who was involved
- Journalistic phrases to make the article more realistic
- Quotes from people involved or witnesses

Q4 Decide whose point of view you are going to write the short story from — it could be from the perspective of just one or two characters. You'll already have the plot from the play so you should flesh it out with extra detail that wouldn't be included in the original play. Some things you could include are:
- private conversations that happen between characters
- inner monologues showing how people feel about the events
- the mannerisms and facial expressions of the characters

The Answers

Page 36 — Writing From Your Point of View

Q1 This is a magazine article and its purpose is to entertain. You should include lots of details about the incident. Keep it chatty — it's for a magazine so it doesn't need to be too formal. You can exaggerate if you want, and you might decide to make it sound funny. Some things to think about are:
• When and where the scary experience took place
• Who was there and who was involved
• Why it was so scary
• What happened afterwards

Q2

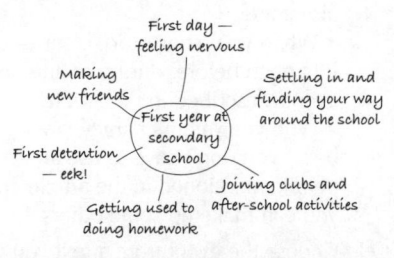

Mind map centred on "First year at secondary school" with branches:
- First day — feeling nervous
- Settling in and finding your way around the school
- Joining clubs and after-school activities
- Getting used to doing homework
- First detention — eek!
- Making new friends

Q3 It's written in the first person (it uses "I") and talks about personal feelings (e.g. "relaxed"). The extract describes what the writer can hear and smell, and includes personal details such as "I'd slept well". It also uses a rhetorical question ("Could this be any more perfect?") to express the writer's opinion.

Q4 This is a short story, so its purpose is to entertain. It needs to be written from your point of view. Make sure you include lots of details to make it personal. Some points you could include are:
• where you went, how long for and how old you were.
• what made it so special
• memories of specific events from the holiday
• things you saw, smelled, ate, felt and heard

Q5 This is a newspaper article, so its purpose is to inform. As it's about your favourite band, it should also be entertaining. Try and include as much information about the band as possible, as well as your personal opinion of them. Some things to think about are:
• when you first heard them
• why you like them so much
• if you've ever been to see them perform and what you thought of it

Section Eight — The Controlled Assessment — English Language

Page 38 — Moving Images

Answer 2: • This part of the answer would get grade B because it has a good range and choice of words. The paragraphs are organised well and the piece offers a clear viewpoint. It suits a film review style. The spelling's good and there is a bit of detail about the acting.
This answer would get a higher grade if it used more ambitious vocabulary, more varied punctuation, and managed to engage more successfully with the reader.

Page 39 — Commissions

Answer 1: • This part of the answer would get grade C because it starts well and takes a personal approach. It's in an article style and there are some good points. The title isn't very imaginative. The spelling's quite good and paragraphs are used. Apostrophes are used and the punctuation's varied and in the right place.
This answer would get a higher grade if it used more varied sentence structures and included more descriptive detail.

Answer 2: • This part of the answer would get grade B as it's written in a good style for an article. It has a light-hearted tone that's suited to the audience. It's original and makes good use of anecdotes and humour. The spelling is right and the words used are not too basic. Speech is included and characters are described. The title sums up the approach of the article nicely.
To get a higher mark, this answer would need to use more complex vocabulary and sentence structures.

Page 40 — Re-creations

Answer 1: • This part of the answer would get grade A because it's original and uses content and themes from the poem. It's well organised and uses paragraphs and headlines. The language is right for a newspaper article. There's an interview and quote included and the spelling's good. Good descriptive words are used.
To get a higher mark, this answer would need to use more varied punctuation and use more writing techniques.

Answer 2: • This part of the answer would get grade B because it uses good language for a travel guide. It's imaginative and paragraphs are used well. The punctuation and spelling are mainly good. It uses some key descriptions from the poem.
This answer would get a higher grade if it used the poem and its ideas more, and used a variety of sentence structures and more complex vocabulary.

Section Nine — The Controlled Assessment — English

Page 42 — Moving Images

Answer 2: • This part of the answer would get grade B because it's confident and has good description, but there isn't quite enough excitement for an adventure film. The spelling and the punctuation are mainly right, and there is a clear story. Paragraphs are used and it sets the scene for the next instalment. There is atmosphere, an exotic location and it could work well for the big screen.
To get a higher mark, this answer needs more visual detail. More varied vocabulary and original ideas would help to improve it.

Page 43 — Prompts and Re-creations

Answer 1: • This part of the answer would get a grade C because it follows on well from the opening line and there has some good descriptions. The spelling is good and it makes good use of paragraphs. It is clear that there is a story developing.
This answer would get a higher mark if it used more interesting vocabulary and a wider range of sentence structures. It could do with some more detail and more links between

The Answers

the ideas to make it clearer what's going on.

Answer 2: • This part of the answer would get grade A* because it creates atmosphere, is exciting and uses detailed description. There is an intriguing story developing. It uses interesting vocabulary. The spelling is accurate and punctuation is varied. The way it's written makes it reflect the action of her hurrying. It's original and there are some creative plot ideas as well as strong feelings shown through emotive language.

Page 44 — Me. Myself. I.

Answer 1: • This part of the answer would get grade A* as it is lively and interesting to read. The spelling and punctuation are good. It makes the reader want to keep reading to learn more. Personal feelings are put across well, with good descriptions of everyday detail. Paragraphs are used properly and there's a good range of punctuation. There's both humour and fear shown.

Answer 2: • This part of the answer would get grade B because it has a lot of varied punctuation and accurate spelling. It describes feelings well and there's a clear idea of how they used to think and how they think now. It has a clear structure and makes good use of paragraphs.
This answer would get a higher grade if it used more interesting vocabulary and descriptive language.

ISBN 978 1 84146 944 7

EWHA42